PUBLIC RELATIONS SECRETS

Unlock the Power of PR and Watch Your Brand Soar

Ray Goodwin

CONTENTS

LIABILITY DISCLAIMER

The information contained within this book is intended for informational purposes only and should not be construed as legal or professional advice. The authors and publishers of this book are not responsible for any losses or damages that may arise from the use of the information contained within.

The reader assumes full responsibility for any decisions made based on the information in this book. The authors and publishers do not endorse any particular method, service or product mentioned in this book and are not responsible for any consequences resulting from their use.

The reader should exercise caution and discretion when making life changing decisions, and should be aware of the risks and potential consequences of their actions. This book is not a substitute for professional or legal advice and should not be relied upon as such.

By reading and using the information in this book, the reader acknowledges and agrees to hold harmless the authors, publishers, and any other parties involved in the creation or distribution of this book from any and all liability, claims, damages, or losses that may arise from their use of the information contained herein.

CHAPTER 1: INTRODUCTION TO PUBLIC RELATIONS

Welcome to Public Relations Secrets, an insider's guide to winning the hearts and minds of your target audience! In today's hyper-connected world, where social media has levelled the playing field, public relations (PR) is more important than ever. Whether you're a small business owner, a nonprofit organization or a large corporation, building and maintaining a positive public image is key to success.

As the author of this book, I've spent many years working in public relations for a variety of clients in various industries. Through my experience, I've come to realize that there are certain secrets to effective PR that every professional should know. That's why I wrote this book – to share those secrets with you.

In these pages, you'll learn how to craft compelling messages that resonate with your target audience; how to leverage social media platforms like Twitter and Instagram for maximum impact; how to build relationships with journalists and bloggers that can help amplify your message; how to respond quickly and effectively in times of crisis; and much more.

But perhaps most importantly, I'll show you how to cultivate a mindset that places authenticity and transparency at the centre of all your PR efforts. Because in today's world, consumers demand honesty from the brands they interact with – and those that fail to deliver risk being left behind.

So whether you're looking to build brand awareness, increase sales or simply connect with your community on a deeper level, Public Relations Secrets has everything you need to succeed in today's competitive marketplace.

Let's get started!

Public relations (PR) is a multifaceted field that involves managing a company's communication with the public. In today's fast-paced world, where social media has become a primary source of news and information, public relations has become an essential part of any business strategy. In this chapter, we will explore the definition and evolution of public relations, the importance of public relations in business, and the role of public relations professionals.

Definition of Public Relations

Public relations is a strategic communication process that builds mutual understanding between an organization and its stakeholders. The aim of public relations is to create a positive image of the organization, reinforce its reputation, and influence its target audience. Public relations is often referred to as earned media, meaning that the coverage is gained through non-paid methods such as press releases, media pitches, and content marketing.

Importance of Public Relations in Business

Public relations is crucial for any business, regardless of size or industry. It helps organizations to build and maintain relationships with their target audience, improve brand recognition, and enhance their reputation. A well-crafted public relations campaign can attract new customers, retain current customers, and increase brand loyalty. Public relations can also help businesses to manage crises and conflicts, and to navigate the often-complex landscape of government regulations.

Evolution of Public Relations

Public relations has come a long way since its inception in the early 20th century. In the past, public relations was largely focused on publicity and media relations. Today, public relations has expanded to include a range of communication channels, such as social media, content marketing, influencer marketing, events, and sponsorships. With the rise of social media, public relations has also become more two-way, allowing organizations to engage with their audiences and receive feedback in real-time.

Types of Public Relations

There are various types of public relations, including internal, external, crisis, government, community, and international relations. Internal public relations involves managing communication within an organization, such as communicating with employees or responding to internal crises. External public relations focuses on communication with external stakeholders, such as customers, investors, and the media. Crisis public relations involves managing communication in the event of a crisis, such as a product recall or a data breach. Government relations involves communicating with government officials and agencies on behalf of an organization. Community relations involve building and nurturing relationships with local communities. International public relations involves managing communication with stakeholders in different countries and cultures.

Role of a Public Relations Professional

A public relations professional plays a vital role in managing an organization's communication with its stakeholders. The role requires a range of skills, including strategic thinking, creativity, and excellent communication skills. A public relations professional must be able to think on their feet and adapt to changing circumstances. They must also be able to build and maintain positive relationships with a range of stakeholders, from journalists and influencers to customers and government officials.

Key Skills for Public Relations Professionals

There are certain skills that are essential for success in a career in public relations. These include strong writing and communication skills, as well as the ability to think creatively and strategically. A public relations professional must also be able to work well under pressure and manage multiple priorities at once. In addition, they must be able to build and maintain relationships, both online and offline.

Ethics in Public Relations

Ethics are of paramount importance in public relations. A public relations professional must operate with transparency and integrity and must always be truthful in their communication. They must also be aware of potential conflicts of interest and must take steps to avoid them. In addition, they must respect the privacy and confidentiality of their stakeholders and must comply with all relevant laws and regulations.

Common Misconceptions about Public Relations

There are many misconceptions about public relations, such as the idea that it is solely focused on spin and manipulation. In reality, public relations is about building mutually beneficial relationships between an organization and its stakeholders.

Another misconception is that public relations is only relevant for large corporations. In truth, public relations is important for businesses of all sizes, from startups to multinational corporations.

CHAPTER 2: UNDERSTANDING THE TARGET AUDIENCE

In the world of public relations, understanding the target audience is essential for crafting effective messages and building successful campaigns. As a public relations professional, one must possess the skills and knowledge to understand who the target audience is and what motivates them to take action. This chapter will explore the importance of understanding the target audience, how to identify their needs and wants, and how to measure success with the target audience.

Defining the Target Audience

The target audience is the group of people that a public relations campaign is designed to reach and influence. The target audience can be defined based on various characteristics such as demographics (age, gender, income, education, etc.), psychographics (personality traits, values, beliefs, attitudes, etc.), geographic location, behavior patterns, and more. Depending on the objectives of a public relations campaign, the target audience can vary widely.

For example, a campaign to raise awareness about a new healthcare product may target women over the age of 40 who will benefit most from the product. Or a campaign to promote a music festival may target millennials and Generation Z who are most likely to attend such events. Whatever the target audience, a public relations professional must have a clear understanding of who they are and what motivates them.

Importance of Understanding the Target Audience

Understanding the target audience is crucial in designing a successful public relations campaign. Without a clear understanding of the target audience, messages may be irrelevant or even worse, may not resonate with the audience. A public relations professional must have a clear understanding of the target audience, including their needs and wants, in order to craft messages that will motivate them to take action.

Identifying the Needs and Wants of the Target Audience

To effectively reach and influence the target audience, one must identify their needs and wants. Needs are those things that are essential for the target audience to fulfill their basic requirements such as food, shelter, safety, and security. Wants to refer to the desires and aspirations of the target audience, such as a desire for status, recognition, or happiness.

Conducting Market Research

Conducting market research is an important tool for identifying the needs and wants of the target audience. This can involve analyzing data from surveys, focus groups, online forums, and social media to gain insights into the target audience's preferences and behaviors. Information such as demographics, preferences, buying habits, and lifestyle choices can help guide the development of a public relations campaign.

Creating Audience Personas

Creating audience personas is another effective way of

understanding the needs and wants of the target audience. Audience personas are fictional representations of the target audience that can help in crafting targeted messages and creating a more personalized approach. These personas can be created based on research and can include details such as age, gender, occupation, income, interests, behaviors, and more.

Developing Messaging Tailored to the Target Audience

After defining the target audience, understanding their needs and wants, and creating audience personas, the next step is to develop messaging that will resonate with the target audience. Effective messaging is tailored to the needs and wants of the target audience and is crafted in a way that will motivate them to take action, whether it be to purchase a product, join a movement, or advocate for a cause.

Building Relationships with the Target Audience

Building relationships with the target audience is essential for establishing trust and credibility. Building relationships can involve engaging with the target audience on social media, providing useful information, responding to feedback, and demonstrating a genuine interest in their needs and wants.

Measuring Success with the Target Audience

Measuring success with the target audience can be done through various methods such as tracking website traffic, monitoring social media engagement, analyzing sales data, and conducting surveys. The goal is to measure the effectiveness of the campaign in terms of reaching and influencing the target audience. Based on the feedback received, adjustments can be made to the campaign to optimize its effectiveness.

In Conclusion

Understanding the target audience is a foundational aspect of public relations. As detailed in this chapter, defining the target audience, identifying their needs and wants, conducting market research, creating audience personas, developing messaging tailored to the target audience, building relationships with the target audience, and measuring success with the target audience are all essential components of crafting a successful public relations campaign.

CHAPTER 3: CRAFTING A MESSAGE

Messaging is an essential component of any public relations campaign. It enables companies to communicate their values, mission, and objectives clearly and succinctly, both internally and externally. Whether you are creating a campaign around a product or service, announcing a new initiative, or managing a crisis, crafting the right message is crucial to achieving your goals.

Elements of a Message

A strong message should be clear, concise, and compelling. It should resonate with your target audience and convey your key messaging points in a memorable way. To achieve this, a message should include the following elements:

❖ Key Messaging Points: These are the main ideas that you want to convey to your audience. They should be easy to remember and capture the essence of what your campaign or initiative is all about.

❖ Tone: The tone of your message should be consistent with your brand's personality and values. It should inspire your audience to take action while also reflecting your organization's values and personality. Whether you are trying to evoke empathy, excitement, or urgency, your tone should be tailored to your audience's needs.

❖ Language: The language that you use should be simple,

yet impactful. It should not be filled with jargon or overly complex terms that your audience may not understand. If your message requires technical terms, be sure to define them in a way that your audience can understand.

❖ Call to Action: Your message should provide a clear call to action, encouraging your audience to take the desired action. Whether it's to subscribe to a newsletter, purchase a product, or support a cause, your call to action should be persuasive and easy to understand.

Guidelines for Crafting a Message

Crafting a message may seem daunting, but there are several best practices that you can follow to make the process more manageable. Here are some guidelines to help you create a persuasive message:

❖ Know Your Audience: Before crafting your message, it's important to understand your audience's needs, values, and pain points. Conducting market research, creating audience personas, and analyzing data can help you gain a better understanding of your target audience.

❖ Stay on Target: Your messaging should be focused on your key messaging points. Avoid discussing unrelated topics or adding irrelevant information that could detract from your message.

❖ Use Storytelling: Storytelling is a powerful tool that can help you create an emotional connection with your audience. Using anecdotes, case studies, or personal stories can help humanize your message and make it more memorable.

❖ Be Creative: Creativity is essential in public relations. Brainstorming with the team, trying new approaches, and experimenting with different methods can help you create a message that grabs your audience's attention.

❖ Test Your Message: Before launching your campaign or initiative, it's essential to test your message to ensure that it resonates with your target audience. A/B testing, focus groups, surveys, or metrics analysis all can be used as tools to test message effectiveness.

Consistency in Messaging

Consistency is key to any successful messaging strategy. Consistent messaging builds trust and reinforces your organization's values and mission. It also makes it easier for your target audience to remember and recall your message. Here are some tips for maintaining consistency in your messaging:

❖ Develop a Messaging Guide: A messaging guide should contain your key messaging points, tone, language, and guidelines on how to convey your message across different channels. This document should be used as a reference by your team and partners to ensure that messages are aligned.

❖ Humanize Your Brand: Your brand's personality should be reflected in your messaging. Using a conversational tone, avoiding overly complicated language, and emphasizing empathy can help humanize your brand and make it relatable to your audience.

❖ Tailor Messages to Different Channels: Your messaging should be adapted to different channels, including social media, email, or press releases. The message should be tailored to the specific channel's format, length, and language.

❖ Ensure Alignment Across Channels: All messages should be aligned across different channels to ensure that there are no discrepancies or conflicting information. This can erode the credibility of your message and damage your reputation.

Tailoring Messages for Different Channels

Different channels require different messaging strategies. What works on social media may not work in a press release or an internal newsletter. Understanding the nuances of different channels can help you create messages that resonate with your audience. Here are some tips for tailoring messages to different channels:

* ❖ Social Media: Social media messages should be short, direct, and engaging. Use visuals, hashtags, and timely content to capture your audience's attention. Tailor your message to the platform, understanding the lengths of messages appropriate for each channel.

* ❖ Press Releases: Press releases should be longer than social media messages, but still concise and focused. They should contain all the information relevant to the announcement or event. Follow the traditional format, including the headline, dateline, lead, body, closing, and contact information section.

* ❖ Email: Email messages should be personalized and tailored to the recipient's interests or needs. They should be concise and clear, conveying the message in the subject line or the first sentence.

* ❖ Internal Communications: Tailoring your message to the internal communications channel is key to get engagement from employees. Messages should be relatable, and it can help to use visual aids such as video, images, or infographics. Make sure messaging is aligned with corporate messaging or mission.

Approaches for Communicating Complex Messages

Communicating a complex message to your audience requires

skill and a strategic approach. Complex messages can result in confusion, a lack of engagement, or inattention, damaging the overall effectiveness of the campaign. To communicate complex messages effectively, the following approaches can be used:

- ❖ Use Analogies: Analogies can illustrate complex concepts in a way that is familiar to your audience. Analogies make it easier for your audience to understand your message and remember it.

- ❖ Create Visual Aids: Visual aids such as infographics, diagrams, videos, or slides can make it easier to convey complex information. Using data visualizations can create a representation of your data that is easier to digest.

- ❖ Simplify Your Messaging: Simplifying a complex message into small digestible bits is the best approach. Use plain language and simplify your content and messaging into smaller chunks of relevant information.

- ❖ Develop a Story: Stories can be used to illustrate complex messages and make them more relatable to the audience. Creating a story around the message, with characters and situations similar to the target audience, makes the audience understand the message more easily.

Testing Messages

Testing messages is critical to ensuring that they resonate with your target audience. It is essential to conduct testing before launching a campaign or initiative. Testing can be done through metrics, surveys, focus groups, or other research methodologies. Here are some ways to test your message:

- ❖ Metrics Analysis: Tracking metrics, such as engagement, click-through rates, or conversion rates can help gauge message effectiveness. Metrics can help determine the message's response rate across different channels.

❖ Focus Groups: Focus groups can provide real-time feedback on your message before launching the campaign or initiative. This feedback can help tailor the message to the target audience's needs or preferences.

❖ Surveys: Surveys can help determine how well your audience understands your message and whether it resonates with them.

Measuring Message Effectiveness

Measuring message effectiveness is essential to determining the success of your campaign or initiative. Monitoring of metrics with target audience engagement, conversion rates, or click-through rates can help measure your message's effectiveness. Here are some ways to measure message effectiveness:

❖ Metrics Analysis: Analyzing metrics can help determine how well your message performed. Metrics, such as click-through rates, conversion rates, website traffic, or engagement, can help determine message effectiveness.

❖ Surveys: Surveys can help determine message stickiness or long-term recall rates.

❖ Interviews: Interviews following the campaign with stakeholders can help determine the effectiveness of the message.

In conclusion, crafting a message is a vital component of any public relations campaign. A message should be clear, concise, and compelling, with strong key messaging points, a consistent tone, and a clear call to action. Testing messages, tailoring messages to different channels, and measuring message effectiveness are all essential to ensuring that your message resonates with your target audience. Through creative approaches and consistency, crafting the right message can help your organization achieve its objectives.

CHAPTER 4: MEDIA RELATIONS

Media relations refer to the relationships built between an organization and journalists. This chapter explains the importance of media relations for modern businesses. It defines the types of media outlets that companies can leverage for publicity, such as broadcasting, print, and digital media. It gives insights on how to build and maintain good relationships with journalists, as well as how to pitch stories to the media successfully. It also discusses crisis communication strategies and how to manage media inquiries effectively. Lastly, the chapter details how to measure the success of media relations as part of a public relations campaign.

Why Media Relations Matter

Media coverage helps businesses reach their target audience by exposing them to a larger audience. This exposure can lead to increased sales, brand recognition, and an overall positive image of the organization. Effective media relations ensure that the story or message a company wants to convey gets to the public in the most powerful way possible. A strategic media relations campaign also helps businesses build relationships and connections with journalists covering their industry or beat.

Types of Media

There are three types of media outlets that organizations can leverage to get their message out: broadcasting, print, and digital media. Broadcasting media includes television and radio, while print media includes newspapers and magazines. Digital media encompasses social media, podcasts, webinars, and blogs.

Building Relationships with Journalists

One of the keys to successful media relations is building positive relationships with journalists. PR professionals should do research on the media outlets that cover their industry or beat to figure out which journalists to target. They can follow journalists on social media, attend industry conferences and events, and participate in media interviews. PR professionals should also provide journalists with timely and relevant stories that will captivate their audience.

Pitching Stories to the Media

The success of the pitch is the difference between gaining interest and coverage and the story getting lost in the shuffle. PR professionals have to be skilled in pitching stories to the media. The pitch should be brief, concise, and relevant. PR professionals must pitch stories that align with what the journalist or outlet does as well as match the given deadlines. Pitching the story to the right person and at the right time can make all the difference in getting media coverage.

Handling Media Inquiries

The main idea of media relations is to maintain positive relationships with journalists. Handling media inquiries prompt journalists to seek quotes, statements, or additional information about a company. It's essential to be professional with journalists and provide accurate information quickly to ensure there are no discrepancies in the story. With the right relationship in place, any news coverage can be an excellent opportunity to communicate the company's brand and values.

Crisis Communication with the Media

In a crisis, timing is everything. When in crisis situations, companies must communicate with the media swiftly and effectively to avoid any form of speculation. In such situations, less is always better than more. Businesses must develop a crisis communication plan that outlines the procedures to follow in case of an emergency or crisis. Having a plan in place allows organizations to face a crisis with poise and confidence, minimizing the risk of damage to the company's reputation.

Measuring Media Relations Success

The success of any PR campaign, including media relations, must be measured to evaluate the effectiveness of the campaign and to adjust future efforts. To track success, PR professionals use a variety of metrics to assess media outreach: audience reach, message delivery, and engagement rates. These metrics determine the impact of media relations on business objectives and help the PR team to adjust the strategy moving forward. Measuring success is essential to gauge if media coverage generates leads, increases sales or traffic to the website, or earns positive reviews.

In conclusion, media relations play a critical role in any business's public relations campaign. They help build professional relationships with journalists and media outlets, increase brand awareness, and ultimately boost growth. PR professionals must understand and apply the principles discussed in this chapter to create quality stories that journalists will cover and build a positive reputation for their clients. The relations that media relations create between organizations and the media are vast and using them fosters greater communication that benefits both parties.

CHAPTER 5:
SOCIAL MEDIA

In today's digital age, social media has become an integral part of public relations. With billions of active users, social media platforms provide PR professionals with an opportunity to reach a large audience, increase brand awareness, and engage with customers in real-time. However, effectively managing social media requires a clear strategy and a thorough understanding of the audience and platform.

Overview of Social Media

Social media refers to digital platforms where users can create and share content and interact with others. This includes platforms like Facebook, Twitter, Instagram, LinkedIn, Pinterest, and Snapchat, among others. With a variety of platforms to choose from, it is important for PR professionals to identify which platform(s) are best for their brand and target audience.

Importance of Social Media in Public Relations

Social media is essential for public relations because it allows brands to connect with their target audience in a direct and authentic way. It provides PR professionals with instant feedback and allows them to respond to customer inquiries and concerns in real-time. Social media also allows brands to showcase their personality and values, increase website traffic, and generate leads.

Types of Social Media Platforms

Each social media platform has its own unique audience and purpose. Therefore, it is important to understand the differences among them to effectively communicate with each audience. Here is a brief overview of the most popular social media platforms:

❖   Facebook: Facebook is the world's largest social media platform, with over two billion active users. It is a great platform for building brand awareness, increasing engagement, and driving website traffic.

❖   Twitter: Twitter is a micro-blogging platform with a limit of 280 characters per tweet. It is great for real-time communication, customer service interactions, and sharing breaking news.

❖   Instagram: Instagram is a photo and video-sharing app that is popular among millennial and Gen Z users. It is great for visual storytelling and creating a visually appealing brand profile.

❖   LinkedIn: LinkedIn is a professional networking platform that is great for B2B companies and thought leaders. It allows users to connect with industry professionals, share industry insights, and promote business-related content.

❖   Pinterest: Pinterest is a visual discovery engine that allows users to discover new products, ideas, and inspirations. It is great for businesses that have visually appealing products, such as fashion, beauty, home decor, and food.

❖   Snapchat: Snapchat is a multimedia messaging app that allows users to send temporary photos and videos. It is popular among Gen Z and young millennials and is great for sharing behind-the-scenes content.

Creating a Social Media Strategy

To effectively manage social media, it is important to have a clear strategy in place. Here are some key steps to consider when creating a social media strategy:

❖ Define Objectives and Goals: Determine what you want to achieve with your social media presence. Are you looking to increase brand awareness, generate leads, or provide customer service?

❖ Identify the Target Audience: It is important to know who your target audience is and what they are interested in. This will help you tailor your content and messaging to their interests.

❖ Choose the Right Platform(s): Choose the social media platform(s) that are most appropriate for your brand and target audience. This will ensure that you are reaching the right people and maximizing your efforts.

❖ Develop a Content Strategy: Develop a content calendar that aligns with your objectives and goals. This will ensure that you are providing consistent and engaging content to your audience.

❖ Allocate Resources: Determine the resources needed to execute your social media strategy, including staffing, content creation, and advertising.

❖ Monitor and Measure Success: Monitor your social media accounts regularly and measure the success of your efforts. This will allow you to adjust your strategy as needed and ensure that you are meeting your objectives and goals.

Best Practices for Social Media Management

To effectively manage social media, there are certain best practices to keep in mind. Here are some key practices to consider:

❖ Be Authentic: Authenticity is key in social media. Brands

should use a human voice and be transparent about their values and personality.

❖ Engage with Your Audience: Social media is a two-way conversation. Interact with your audience by responding to comments and messages and participating in relevant conversations.

❖ Use Visuals: Visuals are more engaging than text alone. Use images, videos, and infographics to make your content more appealing to your audience.

❖ Use Hashtags: Hashtags allow your content to be discovered by a broader audience. Use relevant hashtags to increase visibility and engagement.

❖ Experiment with Content: Don't be afraid to experiment with different types of content, such as short videos, live streams, and user-generated content.

❖ Stay Up-to-Date: Social media is constantly evolving. Stay up-to-date with new trends, features, and algorithm updates to ensure that your content is relevant and effective.

Measuring Social Media Success

Measuring the success of social media efforts is essential to determine how well your strategy is working. Here are some key metrics to consider when measuring social media success:

❖ Reach: Reach is the total number of people who see your content.

❖ Engagement: Engagement is the number of likes, comments, shares, and clicks on your content.

❖ Conversion: Conversion is the number of people who take a specific action, such as making a purchase or filling out a form.

❖   Traffic: Traffic is the number of people who visit your website from social media.

❖   ROI: ROI is the return on investment of your social media efforts, calculated by dividing the revenue generated by the total cost of your social media strategy.

In conclusion, social media is a powerful tool for PR professionals to build brand awareness, engage with customers, and generate leads. By developing a clear strategy and implementing best practices, PR professionals can effectively manage social media and measure their success.

CHAPTER 6: CONTENT MARKETING

In today's digital world, content marketing has become an integral part of any organization's public relations strategy. Content marketing is the process of creating and sharing valuable content to attract and retain a clearly-defined audience with the aim of driving profitable customer action. In this chapter, we'll explore the importance of content marketing in public relations and the steps you can take to develop a successful content marketing strategy.

Importance of Content Marketing in Public Relations

The primary goal of content marketing is to create and distribute content that attracts, engages, and retains a clearly-defined audience. This, in turn, can help businesses establish themselves as industry leaders, build a loyal customer base, and increase brand awareness. For public relations professionals, content marketing is a powerful way to tell the brand's story and increase its online visibility. By sharing high-quality and valuable content, companies can improve their search engine rankings and drive more traffic to their website.

Developing a Content Marketing Strategy

To develop a successful content marketing strategy, you need to start with a clear understanding of your target audience. You need to know who they are, what they want, and how they consume content. Once you have a good idea of your audience, you can start creating content that speaks directly to them.

Types of Content

There are various types of content you can create, such as:

❖ Blog Posts - Blogging is one of the most common forms of content marketing, and for good reason. Blogs provide businesses with a platform to share their thoughts and insights, and to explore topics that they may not have the opportunity to cover elsewhere. Blogging also has the added advantage of helping to boost your search engine rankings which can increase your online visibility.

❖ Infographics - Infographics are visual representations of data or information. They are a great way to convey complex information in a way that is easy to understand and visually appealing.

❖ Videos - Videos are an excellent way to engage your audience, and they are rapidly gaining in popularity. With the rise of platforms like Youtube, Facebook Live, and Instagram Stories, video has become a must-have for any content marketing strategy.

❖ E-books - E-books are detailed, long-form pieces of content that provide in-depth information on a specific topic. They can be used to generate leads, as part of an email marketing campaign or as a valuable resource for your audience.

Creating High-Quality Content

Creating high-quality content is key to the success of your content marketing strategy. High-quality content engages your audience, earns their trust, and encourages them to take action. When creating content, it's important to keep the following in mind:

1. Create content that is relevant to your audience

2. Use visuals to make your content more engaging

3. Write in a conversational tone

4. Make sure your content is well-researched and accurate

5. Don't be afraid to show your personality and sense of humor

Promoting Your Content

Creating great content is only half the battle. Once you have created the content, you need to promote it. Promoting your content means sharing it across all of your marketing channels, including social media, email, and your website. Some strategies that can help you promote your content include:

- ➢ Sharing your content on social media channels
- ➢ Writing guest posts for industry blogs
- ➢ Including links to your content in email marketing campaigns
- ➢ Optimizing your website for SEO

Repurposing Your Content

Another essential part of a successful content marketing strategy is repurposing your content. Repurposing means taking a piece of content and using it in a different format or on a different platform. For example, a blog post can be turned into an infographic, or a video can be transcribed and turned into a blog post. By repurposing your content, you extend its lifespan, and it gives you the opportunity to reach a new audience.

Measuring Content Marketing Success

Finally, it's essential to measure the success of your content marketing efforts. Measuring the success of your content marketing efforts means tracking engagement metrics such as likes, shares, comments, and click-through rates. It's important to monitor these metrics regularly to understand what's working and what's not working and adjust your strategy accordingly.

Conclusion

Content marketing is a powerful and cost-effective way to increase your brand's online visibility and establish yourself as an industry leader. By creating high-quality content that speaks directly to your target audience, you can attract new customers, increase engagement, and drive profitable customer action. Remember that great content is only half the battle, and promotion, repurposing, and measurement are just as important to the success of your content marketing strategy.

CHAPTER 7:
INFLUENCER
MARKETING

In a world where people are bombarded with advertisements and promotional messages at every turn, influencer marketing has emerged as a powerful strategy to cut through the noise and reach target audiences in a more authentic and engaging way. In this chapter, we'll explore what influencer marketing is, how it works, and why it's important in the context of public relations.

What is Influencer Marketing?

Influencer marketing is a collaboration between a brand and an influential person (or people) in their industry or niche to promote a product, service, or message to their followers. This person, the influencer, has built a loyal and engaged following on social media, blogs, or other digital platforms, and can persuade their audience to take action based on their recommendations.

Influencer marketing is often seen as a more authentic form of advertising because it's based on relationships and trust. Rather than a brand blasting a message out to a wide audience, an influencer can introduce a product or service to their followers in a way that feels more personal and genuine.

Why is Influencer Marketing Important in PR?

Influencer marketing has quickly become a vital component of public relations because of the growing importance of social media and the declining effectiveness of traditional advertising. Social media has given influencers a platform to reach millions of people, and consumers are becoming more wary of traditional advertising and more receptive to recommendations from people they trust.

By partnering with influencers, brands can tap into their audiences and gain more exposure for their products or services. Influencers can provide valuable social proof and endorsement to a brand, helping to build credibility and trust with their audiences.

Identifying Influencers

Before embarking on an influencer marketing campaign, it's essential to identify the right influencers for your brand. Simply having a large following does not necessarily make someone an influencer. Factors such as engagement, relevance to your brand, and the authenticity of their content are all important considerations.

To identify potential influencers, start by researching popular blogs, social media accounts, and other digital channels in your industry or niche. Look for people who have a significant and engaged following, who are already talking about your brand or products, and who align with your values and brand personality.

Building Relationships with Influencers

Once you have identified potential influencers, it's time to start building relationships with them. The key is to approach influencers with a clear and specific proposal that aligns with their values and aligns with your brand.

Personalization is critical when building relationships with influencers. Take the time to understand their preferences and tailor your pitch to address their needs and interests. Show an interest in their content and engage with them authentically.

Collaborating with Influencers

When it comes to collaborating with influencers, there are a few different approaches you can take. One option is to offer influencers free products or services in exchange for promotion on their channels. Another approach is to pay influencers for their time and endorsement, either in the form of a flat fee or a percentage of sales.

It's important to be transparent and open about your relationship with influencers and to ensure that any promotion is clearly marked as such. Influencers must disclose any financial or business relationship with brands to their audience to maintain credibility and trust.

Measuring Influencer Marketing Success

Like any other aspect of public relations, measuring the success of influencer marketing is essential to justify the investment and optimize future campaigns. Metrics to track include reach, engagement, website traffic, sales, and ROI.

It's important to define clear objectives and goals at the beginning of a campaign and to track progress against these goals regularly. By regularly assessing the effectiveness of your influencer marketing campaigns, you can fine-tune your approach, identify what's working and what's not, and optimize your investments in the future.

Ethics in Influencer Marketing

As influencer marketing has grown in popularity, so has the scrutiny on the industry's ethics. There has been increasing concern about the transparency and authenticity of influencer marketing, including fake followers, sponsored content that does not distinguish itself as such, and misleading endorsements.

It's essential for public relations professionals to ensure that influencer marketing campaigns follow ethical guidelines and comply with relevant regulations and guidelines. This includes ensuring clear disclosure of any financial or business relationship between influencers and your brand and choosing influencers based on merit and credibility, rather than simply their following size.

Risks and Challenges of Influencer Marketing

Influencer marketing is not without its risks and challenges. One potential challenge is ensuring that influencer content aligns with your brand values and messaging. You must also ensure that any messages delivered by influencers are consistent across other channels.

Another challenge is managing the potential backlash when an influencer campaign goes wrong. It's essential to have a crisis communication plan in place should an influencer post or action go viral and to be prepared to respond quickly and transparently to any negative feedback or backlash.

Conclusion

Influencer marketing has become an essential part of modern public relations, helping brands to reach target audiences authentically and with credibility. With the right approach and a careful eye on ethics and transparency, influencer marketing can be a powerful tool in the modern public relations professional's toolkit.

CHAPTER 8: EVENTS AND SPONSORSHIPS

One of the most effective ways to create buzz around your brand is through events and sponsorships. A well-planned and executed event or sponsorship can generate excitement, increase brand awareness, and drive sales. In this chapter, we will explore the different types of events and sponsorships, how to develop a strategy for them, and how to measure their success.

Overview of events and sponsorships in public relations

Events and sponsorships are a crucial aspect of public relations, as they give a face to your brand and enable you to connect with your target audience in a more personal way. However, events and sponsorships can also be expensive, time-consuming, and resource-intensive. Therefore, it's important to have a clear understanding of their purpose and objectives before embarking on a campaign.

Events can take many forms, ranging from product launches, trade shows, and conferences to charity events, sporting events, and music festivals. Sponsorships, on the other hand, involve providing financial or other support to a third-party event or organization in exchange for brand visibility and exposure. Sponsorships can take the form of naming rights, product placement, or endorsement deals.

Types of events and sponsorships

There are several types of events and sponsorships, each with its unique set of advantages and challenges:

Product launches: These events are designed to grant media access to new products, build anticipation, and generate buzz around the brand.

Trade shows and conferences: These events are a great way to showcase products and services, meet potential customers and partners, and gain valuable industry insights.

Charity events: These events provide an opportunity to give back to the community while boosting brand reputation and goodwill.

Sporting events: These events provide an opportunity to sponsor athletes or teams and access large audiences.

Music festivals: These events provide an opportunity to sponsor artists or stages and reach a diverse demographic.

Developing an event or sponsorship strategy

Before planning an event or sponsorship, it's essential to define your objectives and target audience. What do you want to achieve through an event or sponsorship? Who are you trying to reach, and what interests and needs do they have?

Once you have defined your objectives and target audience, you need to decide on the type of event or sponsorship that will best meet your goals. This involves considering factors such as cost, reach, ROI, and brand fit.

Next, you need to plan the logistics of your event or sponsorship, including selecting a location, booking vendors, designing collateral, and creating a schedule. It's also essential to create a budget and ensure that you have the required resources to execute the plan successfully.

Promoting events and sponsorships

One of the most critical aspects of an event or sponsorship is the promotion that goes into it. A well-executed promotional campaign can generate excitement, attract attendees or participants, and increase brand visibility and reach.

Promotion can take the form of social media posts, email newsletters, paid advertising, influencer partnerships, and media outreach. It's also important to leverage any existing relationships with partners, sponsors, or stakeholders to maximize reach and exposure.

Measuring event and sponsorship success

Measuring the success of an event or sponsorship is crucial to determining whether it achieved the desired objectives and whether it provided a positive ROI. There are several ways to measure the success of an event or sponsorship, including:

❖   Attendance: Measuring the number of attendees or participants can give an indication of interest and the size of the audience reached.

❖   Social media engagement: Measuring likes, comments, shares, and mentions on social media can indicate the level of engagement and interest generated by the event or sponsorship.

❖   Media coverage: Measuring the quantity and quality of media coverage can indicate the reach and effectiveness of the event or sponsorship.

❖   Sales: Measuring the impact on sales can indicate whether the event or sponsorship resulted in a positive ROI.

Managing risks and challenges associated with events and

sponsorships

Events and sponsorships come with several risks and challenges, such as logistical issues, budget overruns, reputational damage, and legal liabilities. Therefore, it's essential to have a comprehensive risk management plan in place to address any potential issues.

One key aspect of risk management is contingency planning, which involves anticipating potential issues and developing protocols to address them. Another key aspect is crisis communication, which involves having a plan in place to disseminate information and manage the fallout from any negative events.

Ethics in events and sponsorships

Events and sponsorships can raise ethical issues, such as conflicts of interest, exploitation of vulnerable populations, and environmental impact. Therefore, it's essential to consider the ethical implications of an event or sponsorship and ensure that it aligns with your brand values and mission.

Conclusion

Events and sponsorships are a powerful tool in the public relations toolbox, enabling brands to connect with their target audience in a more personal way. However, to achieve success, it's crucial to have a clear strategy, adequate resources, and a comprehensive risk management plan in place. By following the guidelines outlined in this chapter, you can maximize the impact of your events and sponsorships and generate positive ROI for your brand.

CHAPTER 9: CRISIS COMMUNICATION

In this chapter, we will be discussing the important role of crisis communication in public relations. No matter how well an organization or business is managed, crises are inevitable. A crisis can be defined as any event that threatens the reputation, operation, or survival of an organization. There are different types of crises, including financial crises, legal crises, natural disasters, cyber-attacks, and product recalls. Regardless of the nature of the crisis, it is crucial for a business to have a well-prepared crisis communication plan to manage the impact of the crisis on its stakeholders.

Importance of Crisis Communication in Public Relations:

The way an organization responds to a crisis can have a significant impact on its reputation, as well as the trust and credibility it holds with stakeholders. In adverse situations, crisis communication can help an organization maintain control of the situation and minimize the impact of the crisis. Effective crisis communication can also help to rebuild and restore trust with stakeholders. If a business does not handle a crisis appropriately, it can lead to loss of revenue, loss of customers, and damage to the organization's reputation.

Types of Crises:

There are different types of crises that can affect an organization.

Some examples include legal crises, financial crises, natural disasters, cyber-attacks, misconduct scandals, product recalls, and more. Each type of crisis presents unique challenges and requires a different approach to crisis communication. Organizations must be prepared to respond to any situation that may threaten their reputation or operations.

Developing a Crisis Communication Plan:

The first step towards preparing for a crisis is to develop a crisis communication plan. This plan outlines the processes and protocols that the organization will follow during a crisis. A crisis communication plan should include the following elements:

- ❖ Crisis Management Team: This team should include key stakeholders within the organization who will be responsible for managing the crisis response.

- ❖ Crisis Communication Protocols: The plan should outline how information will be communicated internally and externally during the crisis.

- ❖ Chain of Command: The plan should outline who is responsible for making decisions during the crisis and who will communicate to different stakeholder groups.

- ❖ Message Development: The plan should outline how the organization will develop messages that are consistent, timely, and appropriate for each stakeholder group.

- ❖ Stakeholder Identification: The plan should identify the different stakeholder groups that will be impacted by the crisis, including employees, customers, shareholders, and the media.

- ❖ Media Relations: The plan should outline how the organization will handle media inquiries during the crisis.

- ❖ Monitoring and Evaluation: The plan should outline

processes for monitoring and evaluating the effectiveness of the crisis communication response.

Strategies for Crisis Communication:

Once a crisis communication plan is in place, the organization should be prepared to implement different strategies for crisis communication. These strategies will vary depending on the nature of the crisis and the stakeholder groups involved. Below are some strategies that organizations can use during a crisis:

❖ Be Transparent: During a crisis, it is important for an organization to be transparent and honest with stakeholders. This means providing them with accurate and timely information about the crisis.

❖ Apologize: If the organization is at fault for the crisis, it is important to apologize and take responsibility for the situation. This can help to rebuild trust with stakeholders.

❖ Communicate Effectively: Effective communication is crucial during a crisis. Organizations should tailor their messaging to different stakeholder groups and use appropriate channels to communicate with them.

❖ Monitor Social Media: Social media can be a powerful tool during a crisis. Monitoring social media can help the organization to understand how stakeholders are reacting to the crisis and ensure that accurate information is being shared.

❖ Provide Support: During a crisis, stakeholders may need support. Organizations should be prepared to provide support to employees, customers, and other stakeholders who may be impacted.

Measuring Crisis Communication Success:

Measuring the success of crisis communication can be challenging. However, it is important to evaluate the effectiveness of the response to identify areas for improvement. Some metrics that can be used to evaluate crisis communication success include:

❖ Media Coverage: This includes the volume and tone of media coverage during the crisis.

❖ Stakeholder Feedback: This includes feedback from stakeholders about the organization's response to the crisis.

❖ Social Media Engagement: This includes the volume and sentiment of social media engagement during the crisis.

❖ Business Continuity: This includes the impact of the crisis on the organization's operations and revenue.

❖ Brand Reputation: This includes the impact of the crisis on the organization's brand reputation with stakeholders.

Conclusion:

Crisis communication is an essential aspect of public relations. Preparing for a crisis and having a well-developed crisis communication plan can help organizations to manage the impact of the crisis on their stakeholders and maintain their reputation. Effective crisis communication requires transparency, honesty, and a willingness to take responsibility for the situation. Measuring the success of crisis communication can help organizations to identify areas for improvement and build better relationships with their stakeholders.

CHAPTER 10: REPUTATION MANAGEMENT

Reputation is everything in business. It can take years to build a good reputation, and just one negative event can tarnish it. Your reputation is how your customers perceive your business, and it can have a significant impact on your success. Reputation management is the process of building, maintaining, and protecting your brand's reputation.

Defining Reputation Management

Reputation management is a proactive approach to managing the perceptions and opinions of your brand. It involves monitoring what people are saying about your brand, responding to negative feedback, and promoting a positive image of your brand. Reputation management starts with understanding your brand's reputation and being proactive in maintaining it.

Importance of Reputation Management

Your brand's reputation can affect your bottom line. A negative reputation can hurt your sales, drive away customers, and damage your brand image. More than ever, customers are researching businesses before making a purchase. A study by BrightLocal found that 88% of customers have read reviews to determine the quality of a local business. Companies with a negative online reputation can lose up to 22% of customers before they even have a chance to make a first impression.

Building a Good Reputation

Building a good reputation requires a proactive approach. The first step is to understand how your brand is perceived by customers. You can do this by conducting surveys and monitoring online reviews. Once you understand your brand's reputation, you can take steps to improve it.

One way to build a good reputation is to be transparent. Customers appreciate honesty, and being upfront about your brand's shortcomings can build trust. Another way to build trust is by providing excellent customer service. Treating customers well and resolving any issues promptly can go a long way in building a positive reputation.

Protecting Your Reputation

Protecting your reputation involves being proactive in monitoring what people are saying about your brand. You can monitor online reviews, social media, and news outlets to stay on top of any negative feedback. Responding to negative feedback quickly and constructively can help mitigate any damage to your reputation.

It's also important to have a crisis communication plan in place. This should include a plan for managing any negative events that could damage your brand's reputation. Having a plan in place can help you respond quickly and effectively to any crisis.

Responding to Negative Feedback

No matter how excellent your customer service is, negative feedback is inevitable. The key is to respond to negative feedback constructively. Responding defensively or ignoring negative feedback can make the situation worse. Instead, respond promptly and offer to resolve any issues. This shows customers that you care about their satisfaction and are willing to take steps to make things right.

Measuring Reputation Management Success

Measuring the success of your reputation management efforts involves monitoring your brand's reputation over time. This can include tracking online reviews, social media mentions, and news articles. You can also conduct surveys to measure customer satisfaction and brand perception. A positive trend over time indicates that your reputation management efforts are working.

Ethics in Reputation Management

Ethics are essential in reputation management. It's important to be honest and transparent with customers and not to engage in any unethical practices such as fake reviews or misleading advertising. Customers appreciate honesty, and being upfront about your brand's shortcomings can build trust.

Risks and Challenges of Reputation Management

One of the biggest risks of reputation management is that an online reputation can be difficult to control. With the prevalence of social media, anyone can share their opinions about your brand, and these opinions can spread quickly. Additionally, there is a risk of overreacting to negative feedback and making the situation worse. It's important to take a measured approach to reputation management and have a plan in place for managing any negative events.

In conclusion, reputation management is a proactive approach to managing your brand's reputation. Building a good reputation takes time and effort, but it is critical to the success of your business. Protecting your brand's reputation involves being proactive in monitoring what people are saying about your business, responding to negative feedback constructively, and having a crisis communication plan in place. Measuring the success of your reputation management efforts involves tracking your brand's reputation over time, monitoring online reviews and social media mentions, and conducting customer surveys. Finally, ethics are essential in reputation management, and it's important to be honest and transparent with customers and avoid any unethical practices.

CHAPTER 11: INTERNAL COMMUNICATION

Internal communication is the backbone of any organization. It refers to the exchange of information within a company, between its employees and management. Effective internal communication is essential for enhancing employee engagement, increasing productivity, and ensuring a smooth functioning of organizational processes.

In this chapter, we will discuss the importance of internal communication in public relations, the different types of internal communication, developing an internal communication strategy, managing internal crises, measuring internal communication success and ethics in internal communication.

Importance of Internal Communication in Public Relations:

Internal communication plays a crucial role in a company's public relations efforts. It is the foundation for creating a cohesive and collaborative work environment. When employees feel informed and involved, they are more likely to become ambassadors for the company. In turn, this enhances the company's reputation and public relations efforts.

Internal communication also helps organizations in crisis management. When employees are aware of what is happening in the company, they can act as advocates and provide support to the company during a crisis. Through regular communication, employees can be informed about the company's values, mission, and objectives. This helps in aligning their work with the company's goals.

Types of Internal Communication:

There are different types of internal communication that organizations use to communicate with their employees. These include:

- ❖ Top-Down Communication - This refers to the flow of information from senior management to employees.

- ❖ Bottom-Up Communication - This refers to the flow of communication from employees to senior management.

- ❖ Lateral Communication - This refers to communication between employees at the same level.

- ❖ Diagonal Communication - This refers to communication that goes across different levels and departments.

Developing an Internal Communication Strategy:

Developing a comprehensive internal communication strategy is crucial for ensuring effective communication within organizations. Here are some of the key steps involved in developing an internal communication strategy:

- ❖ Define Goals - Define the goals and objectives of the internal communication strategy.

- ❖ Identify the Audience - Identify the audience and their communication needs.

- ❖ Develop Key Messages - Develop key messages that align with the company's values, vision, and mission.

❖ Choose Communication Channels - Choose the most appropriate communication channels to reach employees.

❖ Create a Communication Plan - Develop a communication plan that outlines timing, methods, and responsibility for communication.

❖ Implementation - Implement the communication plan and monitor communication effectiveness.

Managing Internal Crises:

Internal crises can happen at any time, and effective internal communication is essential to manage such crises. Here are some steps to follow during internal crises:

❖ Identify the crisis communication team - The crisis communication team should be established before a crisis occurs.

❖ Address the crisis internally - Communicate the crisis internally before going public.

❖ Provide regular updates - Provide regular updates to employees to keep them informed.

❖ Be transparent - Ensure transparency in communication to build employee trust.

Measuring Internal Communication Success:

Measuring the success of internal communication can be challenging but is important for ensuring continuous improvement. Here are some ways to measure internal communication effectiveness:

❖ Employee Feedback - Conduct employee surveys to gather feedback on internal communication.

❖ Tracking Data - Use data to track employee engagement

with internal communication.

❖ Performance Indicators - Use performance indicators to measure the effectiveness of internal communication.

❖ Business Outcomes - Measure the impact of internal communication on business outcomes.

Ethics in Internal Communication:

Ethical considerations are critical when it comes to internal communication. Confidentiality, fairness, and transparency in communication are essential to ensure that employees feel respected and valued. Here are some ethical considerations for internal communication:

❖ Respect Privacy - Respect employees' privacy and protect sensitive information.

❖ Be Transparent - Ensure transparency in communication and avoid misleading employees.

❖ Communicate Ethically - Communicate ethically and avoid dishonesty or manipulation in communication.

In conclusion, internal communication is an essential element of public relations. Creating a culture of effective internal communication is essential for enhancing employee engagement and improving business outcomes. A comprehensive internal communication strategy can help organizations achieve this, and it should be managed with ethics and transparency at its core.

CHAPTER 12: COMMUNITY RELATIONS

As a business, your relationship with the community is extremely important. A negative relationship with the community can make it difficult to conduct business effectively. In contrast, a positive relationship can make the community more receptive to your messages and ultimately lead to more business opportunities. In this chapter, we will explore what community relations are and how you can improve your relationship with the community.

Definition of Community Relations

Community relations is the process of building positive relationships between a business or organization and the communities in which it operates. It involves engaging with community members, organizations, and leaders to understand their needs, concerns, and interests. The ultimate goal of community relations is to create a mutually beneficial relationship that helps both the business and the community thrive.

Importance of Community Relations in Public Relations

Community relations is an important component of public relations because it helps businesses build trust and credibility with the people who live and work in the community. When a business engages with the community in a positive way, people are more likely to view the business as a good corporate citizen. This can lead to increased loyalty among customers and increased support from the community. Positive community relations can also help a business navigate potential crises more effectively, as the community may be more willing to listen to and trust the business's message.

Building Relationships with Communities

The first step in building a positive relationship with the community is to engage with community members. This may involve attending community events, participating in community organizations and groups, and establishing open lines of communication with community leaders. It's important to take the time to understand the issues that are important to the community, as well as the cultural norms and values that shape the community.

Developing a Community Relations Strategy

Once you have established a relationship with the community, it's important to develop a community relations strategy that outlines how you will engage with the community. This may involve developing targeted messaging that speaks to the needs and concerns of the community, organizing community events or initiatives, or establishing partnerships with key community organizations.

Communicating with Community Members

Effective communication is key to building positive community relations. It's important to establish clear and transparent communication channels that allow community members to provide feedback and share their concerns. This may involve creating a dedicated community feedback line or establishing a community liaison who can serve as a point of contact for community members.

Managing Community Crises

When your business is faced with a crisis that impacts the community, it's important to respond quickly and effectively. This may involve providing timely and accurate information to the community, as well as establishing a plan to address the root cause of the crisis. It's also important to be transparent and honest with the community, even if the situation is difficult.

Measuring Community Relations Success

Measuring the success of your community relations efforts can be challenging, but it's important to track key metrics that can help you understand the impact of your outreach efforts on the community. This may involve tracking the number of community events you attend, the number of community partnerships you establish, or the level of engagement you receive on social media.

Ethics in Community Relations

Just as in other areas of public relations, it's important to approach community relations with a commitment to ethical behavior. This may involve being transparent about your intentions and goals, respecting the cultural norms and values of the community, and being responsive to the needs and concerns of community members.

In conclusion, community relations are incredibly important for any business seeking to build a positive reputation and create opportunities for growth. By taking the time to understand the community, developing a targeted strategy, and communicating openly and honestly, businesses can build strong relationships with the people who live and work in the community. This can ultimately lead to increased trust, increased support, and increased business opportunities.

CHAPTER 13: GOVERNMENT RELATIONS

Government relations encompass building and maintaining relationships with various levels of government officials, from elected representatives to regulatory agencies. These relationships are important for businesses that want to have a voice in decisions that affect their industry. However, it can be challenging to navigate the complex regulatory landscape, which is why a solid government relations strategy is essential.

What is Government Relations?

Government relations, also referred to as lobbying, involves interacting with government officials to influence the development of public policies and laws that impact a company or industry. It is the process of building and maintaining relationships with lawmakers, regulators, and other government officials to achieve business goals.

Businesses that engage in government relations aim to shape public policies and legislation that affect their operations. It can involve communicating with government officials to advocate for specific policy positions and priorities that are beneficial to the company. The goal of government relations is to influence the decision-making process in favor of the company or industry.

Importance of Government Relations in Public Relations

Government relations are vital to public relations because government policies impact the companies and industries operating within the respective nations. Companies that do not engage in government relations risk being left out of the decision-making process. Also, they may face policy or regulatory decisions that adversely affect their operations.

In contrast, companies that engage in government relations proactively can help shape policymaking in a way that is favorable to their interests and goals. They can also manage regulatory risks that may occur in their industry. As a result, businesses with robust government relations programs are often more successful in navigating the regulatory landscape.

Building Relationships with Government Officials

Building relationships with government officials is not easy; it requires dedication and patience. But once established, these relationships can provide the necessary support when a company faces challenges or needs to advocate on policy positions.

To build relationships with government officials, it is essential to understand their interests and priorities. Know their positions on critical issues and understand how their objectives align with your company goals. Reach out to officials through various avenues, such as public meetings and events, phone calls, and email.

Developing a Government Relations Strategy

To develop an effective government relations strategy, businesses must first identify their policymakers and key decision-makers. These individuals must be broken down by local, state, and federal levels of government.

The next step is to establish policy priorities based on the company's needs and interests. These priorities should align with the policymakers' interests, which can be identified through public statements and other means of communication.

Communicating with Government Officials

Companies seeking to advocate for their policy positions must understand how to communicate effectively with government officials. Communication can take many forms, from face-to-face meetings to written communications.

Understanding the preferred method of communication for the government official is critical. For instance, some may prefer face-to-face interactions with lobbyists, while others prefer written briefs or public comments.

Managing Government Crises

Given the potential for regulatory and policy changes, government relations professionals must be prepared to manage government crises. This can involve proactive measures, such as lobbying for favorable legislation or regulations. Alternatively, it could involve reactive measures, such as managing public criticism or legal challenges to new regulations.

Measuring Government Relations Success

Companies should track the outcome of government relations efforts to ensure they are achieving their goals and objectives. This can involve tracking the progress of legislation or regulations, the level of engagement with policymakers, and changes in policies that are favorable to the company or industry.

Additionally, it is necessary to measure how the company's government relations activities impact the company's bottom line, such as the increase in revenues or avoidance of regulatory fines.

Ethics in Government Relations

The importance of ethics in government relations cannot be overstated. Companies must engage in government relations activities that are transparent, honest, and legal. Giving any gifts or undue influence on government officials can result in severe consequences.

Also, it is essential to have robust policies and procedures for compliance with the laws and regulations governing government relations activities.

Conclusion

An effective government relations strategy can pave the way for companies to succeed in a complex regulatory environment. Businesses that engage in government relations are better equipped to navigate the regulatory landscape while advocating for policies that support their operations.

The government relations process requires dedication, patience, and effective communication skills to build and maintain relationships with policymakers. Companies that understand the importance of government relations and have a robust strategy in place will be better prepared to manage crises, advocate for desired policies, and ultimately achieve success in their industries.

CHAPTER 14:
INTERNATIONAL
PUBLIC RELATIONS

Globalization has led to an increase in international business and trade, which means a greater need for international public relations. International public relations refer to the practice of managing relationships and communication with stakeholders across different countries and cultures. In this chapter, we will explore the importance of international public relations and the key considerations that come with managing global public relations efforts.

Overview of International Public Relations

International public relations involve managing communication and relationships with stakeholders in multiple countries and cultures. International public relations practitioners are responsible for promoting their organization's image, reputation, and product or service offerings globally. As companies expand their reach into more countries and markets, the importance of international public relations becomes more critical.

International public relations can help companies maintain a positive image and reputation, develop relationships with international stakeholders, and increase market share in new markets. By understanding the cultural nuances and communication styles of different countries, international public relations professionals can develop effective communication strategies that resonate with their target audiences.

Importance of International Public Relations

The globalization of markets has led to a significant increase in the need for international public relations. As companies expand their reach into new markets, the demand for effective communication strategies that resonate with audiences from different countries and cultures becomes more important. International public relations helps companies build strong relationships and reputation with international stakeholders, which can lead to increased brand awareness and revenue.

For example, multinational companies like Coca-Cola and Nike have established themselves as global brands by using effective international public relations strategies. These companies have tailored their communication strategies to resonate with local audiences in different countries, leading to an increase in sales and market share.

Cultural Differences in Public Relations

When developing an international public relations strategy, it is important to understand the cultural differences between countries. Cultural differences can affect how messages are received, the communication channels used, and even the timing and tone of messages. Understanding these differences is critical to developing effective communication strategies that resonate with audiences from different cultures.

For example, in some cultures, direct communication is considered rude and disrespectful, while in others, it is considered a sign of honesty and respect. Tone and humor also vary significantly across cultures, as do communication styles and social norms. Understanding these differences can help international public relations professionals develop communication strategies that are appropriate for different cultures.

Developing an International Public Relations Strategy

Developing an international public relations strategy involves identifying key stakeholders across different countries and cultures and developing communication strategies that resonate with them. To develop an effective international public relations strategy, it is important to conduct research on local cultures and communication styles to develop messages that are appropriate and engaging for local audiences.

International public relations professionals must identify the communication channels that are most effective in different countries and cultures. For example, social media platforms that are popular in the United States may not be as effective in other countries, so it is important to identify social media channels that are popular in each country.

Localizing Messages for Different Cultures

To effectively communicate with international stakeholders, it is important to tailor messages to resonate with local audiences. This can involve translating messages into different languages and adapting messages to reflect cultural norms and values.

Localization also involves adapting communication styles and channels to align with local cultural practices. For example, in some countries, face-to-face meetings are preferred over email or phone communication, so it is important to understand these differences when developing an international public relations strategy.

Building Relationships with International Stakeholders

Building relationships with international stakeholders is another critical aspect of international public relations. This involves identifying key stakeholders in each country and developing communication strategies that resonate with them. Building relationships with stakeholders can help companies expand their reach, increase brand awareness, and develop new business opportunities.

To build relationships with international stakeholders, it is important to understand their needs and values. This involves conducting research on local cultures, communication styles, and social norms, as well as identifying the communication channels that are most effective in each country.

Measuring International Public Relations Success

Measuring the success of international public relations efforts can be challenging, as it involves measuring the effectiveness of communication strategies across different cultures and countries. To effectively measure the success of international public relations efforts, it is important to identify key performance indicators (KPIs) that are relevant to each country and communication channel.

Some common KPIs for international public relations include media coverage, website traffic, social media engagement, and sales revenue. These metrics can help international public relations professionals evaluate the effectiveness of their communication strategies and identify areas for improvement.

Risks and Challenges of International Public Relations

Managing international public relations efforts can present significant risks and challenges, particularly when dealing with cultural differences and language barriers. Miscommunications and misunderstandings can have significant consequences for a company's reputation and brand image.

Managing these risks involves conducting research on local cultures and communication styles and developing communication strategies that are appropriate and engaging for local audiences. It also involves developing crisis communication plans that can be quickly deployed in the event of a crisis or miscommunication.

Conclusion

International public relations is a critical aspect of managing a successful global business. By understanding the cultural differences and communication styles of different countries, international public relations professionals can develop effective communication strategies that resonate with their target audiences. Building strong relationships with international stakeholders can help companies increase brand awareness, expand their reach, and develop new business opportunities. However, managing international public relations efforts can present significant risks and challenges, so it is important to develop effective crisis communication plans and evaluate the effectiveness of communication strategies on an ongoing basis.

CHAPTER 15: MEASUREMENT AND EVALUATION

Measurement and evaluation play a crucial role in public relations as they help professionals understand the effectiveness of their strategies and tactics. Without measurement and evaluation, it's impossible to determine whether a campaign has been successful or not and what can be improved in future efforts. In this chapter, we'll discuss the importance of measurement and evaluation, the types of tools available, and how to set objectives and goals.

Definition of measurement and evaluation

Measurement involves collecting and analyzing data that represents the performance of a campaign or initiative in an effort to better understand its impact and effectiveness. Evaluations are assessments that are conducted based on the data gathered to determine whether the campaign objectives were met or not.

Importance of measurement and evaluation in public relations

Measurement and evaluation are essential components of any successful public relations campaign. Without these, it's impossible to know if your efforts are having the desired impact. By conducting regular measurement and evaluation, however, you can assess exactly what's working and what's not, allowing you to make appropriate changes to your methods to ensure the next campaign is even more successful than the last.

Types of measurement and evaluation tools

There are several types of measurement and evaluation tools available, each of which can be used in a variety of ways:

❖ Media coverage measurement tools: These tools are designed to track media coverage volume and tone across different channels, both traditional and digital, to help gauge overall exposure generated by a public relations campaign.

❖ Social media engagement measurement tools: These tools are used to track the impact of social media campaigns by analyzing audience engagement, follower growth, and overall social media influence.

❖ Website traffic and conversion rate measurement tools: These tools chiefly help monitor website traffic patterns, page views, and user behavior, thereby providing essential insights into how website visitors are interacting with the contents of your site. This is important information to track since conversion rates can affect your business's bottom line.

❖ Overall campaign effectiveness measurement tools: These types of evaluation tools provide a comprehensive assessment of a campaign's effectiveness by measuring key metrics across all available channels.

Setting objectives and goals for measurement and evaluation

Before you can begin to measure and evaluate a PR campaign, you must first establish clear objectives and goals. These could include items such as increasing brand awareness, growing social media followers, driving website traffic, or even simply maintaining a positive brand image.

Once you have established these objectives, you can then set specific goals that are unique to each objective. For instance, if your objective is to increase brand awareness, your goals may include achieving a certain level of media coverage, social media impressions, and website traffic.

Measuring media coverage

Measuring media coverage involves tracking and recording all mentions of your brand that appear in articles, news stories, and other media outlets. Tools like Muck Rack and Cision are useful for providing detailed analytics pertaining to media coverage, showing you information like where and when articles were published, which media outlets picked up the story, and how that coverage stacks up compared to your competition.

Measuring social media engagement

Social media measurement tools provide a snapshot of your social media audiences' overall engagement with your brand, highlighting details like follower growth, social media reach, and the level of overall engagement on each of your social media platforms. These tools can also provide comprehensive reports on your top-performing posts, which can give you valuable insights into what messages are resonating most strongly with your audience.

Measuring website traffic and conversion rates

Google Analytics is the most commonly used web analytics platform, providing an in-depth look at how website visitors engage with your site and how that impacts your business. The tool tracks everything from user demographics to user behavior to website conversion rates, giving you the information you need to optimize your website and ensure the best possible user experience.

Measuring overall campaign effectiveness

Overall campaign effectiveness tools provide a holistic perspective on campaign performance, measuring key metrics across multiple channels to identify which strategies are working and which aren't. These tools can be useful in clarifying your overall return on investment (ROI) and assessing the overall effectiveness of your PR campaign(s).

Conclusion

Measurement and evaluation are critical aspects of public relations, providing the data needed to gauge the overall effectiveness of your campaigns and identify areas for improvement. By using a variety of measurement and evaluation tools, setting clear objectives and goals, and assessing performance on an ongoing basis, you can ensure your PR efforts are always targeted, effective, and impactful.

CHAPTER 16: BUDGETING AND RESOURCE ALLOCATION

Budgeting and resource allocation are critical components of any successful public relations campaign. In this chapter, we will discuss how to develop a budget and resource allocation plan and effectively manage them to achieve your campaign objectives.

Overview of budgeting and resource allocation in public relations

Before you start any public relations campaign, it's essential to determine the resources and budget you will need to make it a success. The budget will help you estimate the costs of the campaign, which will include salaries, equipment, materials, and other expenses that will be incurred. Resource allocation, on the other hand, informs you of the staff and equipment you'll need to make the whole campaign a success.

Developing a budget and resource allocation plan

To develop a budget and resource allocation plan for your public relations campaign, follow these steps:

❖ Step 1: Define your campaign goals - Before you start developing a budget or allocating resources, you need to have a clear goal in mind for your public relations campaign. This will enable you to determine the amount of money and resources you will need to achieve your objectives.

❖ Step 2: Identify necessary resources - Once you've defined your campaign goals, you can start to identify the resources that you'll need to achieve those goals. These may include equipment, personnel, materials, including software.

❖ Step 3: Estimate costs - After identifying the resources you will need, determine how much it will cost to acquire them. Be sure to include every cost that is relevant to your campaign, such as printing, advertising, travel expenses, and more.

❖ Step 4: Allocate resources - With your resources identified and costs estimated, the next step is to assign specific resources to each goal. Allocate resources based on the goals you want to achieve and the resources available.

❖ Step 5: Create a budget - Once you've allocated resources, you can now create a comprehensive budget for the entire campaign. Your budget should show all expenditures, including any contingencies.

Identifying necessary resources

When planning your budget and resource allocation, it's essential to determine the specific resources you will need to run the campaign effectively. These resources are usually divided into two broad categories – human and non-human resources.

Human resources encompass the team members who will work on the campaign. The team may include public relations professionals, writers, designers, event planners, and more, depending on what your budget allows.

Non-human resources include any assets you will need to purchase or rent to accomplish your campaign goals. This may include equipment such as laptops, cameras, microphones, printers, and other hardware and software tools.

Allocating resources effectively

Effective resource allocation is key to ensure that the campaign achieves its goals efficiently. As outlined in the previous section, it's wise to allocate resources based on the goals you want to achieve. For instance, if your campaign goal is to increase your company's social media engagement, allocate more resources to social media management, such as hiring professionals with expertise in that area.

It's also essential to ensure that resource allocation is flexible enough to respond to unexpected changes and updates during the campaign's timeline. Therefore, outline a clear plan for how to re-allocate resources in case of unforeseen circumstances.

Managing budgets and resources

Once the campaign has commenced, it's essential to keep track of the budget and resources to ensure they don't go overboard. Set up a system to monitor all expenditure and keep track of the campaign's progress as it rolls on.

Part of effective resource management includes responsibility and accountability. Ensure that all team members know their role in the campaign and what is expected of them to keep within the budget and effectively utilize resources. Regular progress reports should also be put in place to evaluate and keep up with the campaign's performance.

Measuring return on investment

Measure ROI to determine these inflows' relation to the resources you allocated for the campaign. Measuring ROI is an essential metric since it helps identify what works and what doesn't work for future campaigns.

To measure ROI, you should evaluate the return on investment of each component of the campaign. This evaluation should include metrics such as website traffic, social media engagement, sales, leads, and revenue generated from the campaign. Analyzing these metrics will help you evaluate the success of the campaign, make any necessary adjustments, and plan for future campaigns.

Conclusion

Budgeting and resource allocation are core parts of any public relations campaign. By accurately developing a budget strategy, allocating resources towards specific goals, being accountable, and keeping abreast of return on investment, you can effectively carry out a successful campaign. A solid budget and resource allocation plan that is effectively managed and measured will drive the successful execution of any public relations campaign.

CHAPTER 17: CAREER DEVELOPMENT IN PUBLIC RELATIONS

Public relations is a fast-paced and exciting industry that offers many rewarding career opportunities. In this chapter, we will explore the skills and qualifications needed for public relations careers, the importance of networking and building professional relationships, advancing in a public relations career, opportunities for continuing education and professional development, and ethics in public relations careers. We will also discuss strategies for balancing work and personal life.

Skills and Qualifications Needed for Public Relations Careers

To succeed in a public relations career, you will need a strong background in communication, marketing, and business. Excellent writing and verbal communication skills are a must, as is the ability to think critically and strategically. You should also be creative, resourceful, and able to work well under pressure.

Most employers require a bachelor's degree in public relations, journalism, marketing, or a related field. A master's degree can be beneficial for advancing in the field or specializing in a particular area of public relations. Professional certifications, such as the Accreditation in Public Relations (APR) or the International Association of Business Communicators (IABC), can also demonstrate your commitment to the profession and help you stand out to potential employers.

Networking and Building Professional Relationships

Networking is a critical part of building a successful career in public relations. It can help you identify potential job opportunities, learn about industry trends and best practices, and connect with professionals who can serve as mentors or references.

There are many ways to network in the public relations industry, including attending conferences, joining professional associations, participating in online forums and social media groups, and reaching out to professionals for informational interviews. Building relationships with journalists, influencers, and other stakeholders can also be beneficial, as it can help you stay connected to the broader industry and identify opportunities for collaboration or partnership.

Advancing in a Public Relations Career

As you progress in your public relations career, you may have the opportunity to take on more significant responsibilities or specialize in a specific area of public relations, such as media relations, crisis communication, or reputation management. To advance in your career, you will need to demonstrate a track record of excellent work, build your professional network, and continue to develop your skills and knowledge.

Opportunities for Continuing Education and Professional Development

Continuing education and professional development are essential for staying competitive in the public relations industry. There are many ways to continue learning, including attending workshops and seminars, pursuing advanced degrees, reading industry publications, and participating in online training or certification programs.

Many professional associations also offer opportunities for continuing education and professional development, including webinars, conferences, and networking events. These events can help you stay up-to-date on the latest trends and best practices in the field and connect with other professionals who can offer valuable insights and advice.

Ethics in Public Relations Careers

Ethics are a critical component of public relations careers. As public relations professionals, we have a responsibility to be honest, transparent, and ethical in all of our communications and interactions with stakeholders. This means avoiding conflicts of interest, disclosing any potential biases or affiliations, and respecting the privacy and rights of others.

Balancing Work and Personal Life

While public relations can be a demanding and fast-paced career, it is essential to find a healthy work-life balance. This means setting realistic expectations for workload and prioritizing self-care, including exercise, leisure activities, and spending time with family and friends.

One helpful strategy for finding a balance between your personal and professional life is to establish clear boundaries around work and downtime. This might mean turning off your work phone or email during off-hours, delegating tasks to others, or taking regular breaks during the workday to recharge.

Conclusion

A career in public relations can be challenging but rewarding. By developing the right skills and qualifications, building strong professional relationships, continuing to learn and grow, prioritizing ethics and integrity, and finding a healthy work-life balance, you can build a successful and fulfilling career in this exciting industry.

CHAPTER 18: TRENDS AND EMERGING TECHNOLOGIES IN PUBLIC RELATIONS

The world of public relations is constantly evolving, and the emergence of new technologies is changing the way that organizations communicate with their audiences. In this chapter, we will explore some of the most notable trends and emerging technologies in public relations and discuss the implications and opportunities they present for the industry.

Artificial Intelligence and Machine Learning in Public Relations

Artificial intelligence (AI) and machine learning are transforming many industries, and public relations is no exception. For example, AI-powered tools can monitor social media conversations and news articles in real-time, providing insights and data that enable PR professionals to make informed decisions about their campaigns. Machine learning algorithms can also analyze data to identify key influencers in a particular industry, enabling PR professionals to tailor their outreach efforts accordingly.

Another key application of AI in public relations is the use of chatbots and virtual assistants. Chatbots can provide quick responses to common questions, freeing up PR professionals to focus on more complex inquiries and issues. Virtual assistants, on the other hand, can perform tasks like scheduling appointments, sending emails, and managing media contacts, streamlining the workflow for PR teams.

Virtual Reality and Augmented Reality in Public Relations

Virtual reality (VR) and augmented reality (AR) are also gaining traction in the public relations world. VR can be used to create immersive experiences that transport audiences to different locations, such as a virtual tour of a new hotel or resort. AR, on the other hand, can be used to enhance real-world experiences by overlaying digital information onto physical objects or environments, such as a museum exhibit.

One of the most promising applications of VR and AR in public relations is the ability to bring events and experiences to audiences who are unable to attend in person. For example, a virtual reality livestream of a conference or product launch can enable people from all over the world to participate and engage with the event in real-time.

Chatbots and Messaging Apps in Public Relations

As mentioned earlier, chatbots are becoming a popular tool for automating certain tasks in public relations. In addition to providing basic customer service and support, chatbots can also help PR professionals manage media inquiries and monitor social media conversations.

Messaging apps like WhatsApp and Facebook Messenger are also becoming important communication channels for PR teams. These apps enable PR professionals to reach audiences in a more personal and direct way, and they also provide opportunities for two-way communication and engagement.

Wearables and Internet of Things in Public Relations

The rise of wearable technology and the Internet of Things (IoT) is also opening up new opportunities for public relations. For example, wearable devices like smartwatches can be used to deliver personalized messages and notifications to users, enabling PR teams to deliver targeted content directly to their target audiences.

IoT devices like smart speakers and home automation systems can also be used to deliver branded content and messaging to consumers. For example, a company that sells kitchen appliances could create a voice-activated recipe assistant that provides cooking tips and product recommendations to users.

Video and Live Streaming in Public Relations

Video content and live streaming are increasingly popular in the world of public relations, and for good reason. Video is a powerful storytelling medium that enables organizations to convey complex ideas and emotions in a visual and engaging way.

Live streaming, in particular, has exploded in popularity in recent years, thanks to platforms like Facebook Live and YouTube Live. Live streaming enables organizations to connect with their audiences in real-time, and it also provides opportunities for engagement and interactivity.

Measuring the Effectiveness of Emerging Technologies in Public Relations

As with any new technology or trend, it is important to measure the effectiveness of these emerging tools and techniques in public relations. One way to do this is by setting clear goals and objectives for each campaign and monitoring key metrics like engagement, reach, and sentiment.

It is also important to test different approaches and strategies to see what works best for your target audience and your organization. A/B testing, for example, can help you determine which messaging or content resonates best with your audience.

Risks and Challenges of Using Emerging Technologies in Public Relations

While the potential benefits of emerging technologies in public relations are clear, there are also risks and challenges that must be considered. One of the biggest risks is the potential for technology failures or glitches, which could lead to negative publicity or damage to an organization's reputation.

The ethics of using certain emerging technologies, such as AI-powered chatbots and virtual assistants, must also be considered. For example, using chatbots to impersonate human customer service representatives could be seen as deceptive or unethical.

Finally, it is important to remember that not all emerging technologies will be a good fit for every organization or campaign. It is important to consider factors like budget, resources, and target audience when deciding which tools and techniques to incorporate into your PR strategy.

In conclusion, the world of public relations is constantly evolving, and emerging technologies are playing an increasingly important role in shaping the way organizations communicate with their audiences. While there are risks and challenges associated with using these tools, the potential benefits are clear, and organizations that are able to harness the power of these technologies will be well-positioned to succeed in the ever-changing world of PR.

CHAPTER 19: CASE STUDIES IN PUBLIC RELATIONS

Public relations are a constantly evolving field, and strategies that were once successful may no longer be effective in today's digital landscape. That's why studying case studies can be an excellent way to learn from both successful and failed campaigns and identify best practices. In this chapter, we will examine several case studies to gain a better understanding of public relations in action.

The Power of Storytelling: Coca-Cola's "Share a Coke" Campaign

In 2011, Coca-Cola launched the "Share a Coke" campaign, which replaced the brand name on bottles and cans with more than 1,000 popular first names. The goal of the campaign was to engage consumers and encourage them to share a Coke with friends and family members.

The campaign was an overwhelming success and resulted in a 2.5% increase in sales volume, which was the first growth the brand had seen in a decade. The campaign also generated more than 1 billion impressions on social media and increased Coca-Cola's social media following by 25%. But how did Coca-Cola achieve such remarkable success?

At the heart of the campaign was a simple concept that resonated with consumers – the idea of sharing. Coca-Cola understood that people love to share things with others, and the campaign tapped into that desire by creating a personal connection between the brand and its customers. By placing people's names on Coke bottles, the campaign personalized the brand and made it feel more relatable.

Another key element of the campaign was its emphasis on storytelling. Coca-Cola told the stories of real people who shared a Coke and created an emotional connection with its customers. The brand utilized social media to encourage people to share their own stories with the hashtag #ShareACoke, further reinforcing the importance of storytelling in public relations.

The Role of Influencers: Adidas' "Run for the Oceans"

In 2018, Adidas launched its "Run for the Oceans" campaign, which aimed to raise awareness about marine plastic pollution and encourage people to participate in a virtual run. The campaign partnered with Parley for the Oceans; a nonprofit organization dedicated to protecting marine ecosystems.

One of the keys to the campaign's success was its use of influencers, specifically athletes and social media personalities, to promote the event. Adidas partnered with athletes such as David Beckham and Lionel Messi, as well as social media personalities with large followings, maximizing the reach and impact of the campaign.

The virtual run allowed people from all over the world to participate in the event, and participants were encouraged to track their runs using the Runtastic app. For every kilometer run, Adidas pledged to donate $1 to the Parley Ocean School, a program that educates young people about ocean preservation.

The campaign was a massive success, with more than 2 million people participating in the virtual run and generating over 12 million kilometers run. The campaign also resulted in a

15% increase in Adidas' social media followers and garnered widespread media attention.

The campaign's success was due in part to its use of influencers, who helped to raise awareness about the event and encourage people to participate. By partnering with Parley for the Oceans, Adidas also aligned itself with a cause that resonated with its target audience and demonstrated the power of cause-related marketing in public relations.

Learning from Failure: Pepsi's "Live for Now" Campaign

In 2017, Pepsi released its "Live for Now" campaign, which aimed to position the brand as a facilitator of social unity and harmony. The campaign featured Kendall Jenner, a popular model and reality TV star, joining a protest and offering a can of Pepsi to a police officer, which many viewers found tone-deaf and insensitive.

The commercial was widely criticized and sparked backlash across social media, with many accusing Pepsi of trivializing social justice movements and co-opting the struggle for racial equality. The company was forced to pull the ad and issue an apology, which demonstrated the importance of considering the potential impact of a campaign on the broader social and political context.

The failure of the "Live for Now" campaign highlights the need for companies to be careful and thoughtful in their public relations efforts. It's essential to listen to feedback from customers and stakeholders to ensure that campaigns are responsive to the needs and values of the target audience.

Conclusion

Public relations is a complex field that requires a deep understanding of the target audience, effective messaging, and a variety of channels to reach them. By studying successful and failed campaigns, we can learn from both best practices and mistakes to improve our own public relations efforts.

The case studies we examined in this chapter demonstrate the power of storytelling, the impact of cause-related marketing, and the role of influencers in promoting events and campaigns. They also remind us of the importance of careful planning and consideration of broader political and social contexts in shaping public relations efforts.

CHAPTER 20: CONCLUSION AND FUTURE OF PUBLIC RELATIONS

Now that we have covered a wide range of topics related to public relations, it's important to recap everything we have learned and understand where the field is headed in the future.

Public relations has evolved significantly over the years, from being solely focused on media relations to encompassing a range of tactics and strategies designed to build and maintain relationships with various audiences. We have explored the importance of understanding the target audience, crafting a compelling message, leveraging social media and influencer marketing, managing events and crises, and measuring the success of public relations campaigns.

As we look to the future, it's clear that the field of public relations will continue to evolve rapidly. Technology, particularly artificial intelligence and machine learning will play an increasingly important role in developing targeted messaging and measuring the effectiveness of campaigns. We are already seeing chatbots and messaging apps being used to communicate with audiences more effectively, and virtual and augmented reality is being leveraged to create immersive experiences.

It's critical for public relations professionals to stay up-to-date on emerging trends and technologies and be willing to adapt their strategies and tactics accordingly. As the field becomes more complex and competitive, it's important to continue learning and growing as a professional.

In addition, ethics will continue to be a critical component of public relations, particularly with the rise of influencer marketing and the potential for negative consequences if not handled correctly. Maintaining transparency, honesty, and integrity in all communications with stakeholders will be essential for building trust and credibility.

Finally, while the future of public relations may be uncertain, one thing is clear: its importance in business will only continue to grow. As companies compete for attention and trust in an increasingly crowded and noisy marketplace, the skills and strategies of public relations professionals will be instrumental in helping them stand out and make a positive impact.

So, as we wrap up this book, I encourage you to continue learning, growing, and pushing the boundaries of what's possible in public relations. The future is bright, and I'm excited to see what it holds for our field.

Final Thoughts

Thank you for taking the time to read Public Relations Secrets. I hope that through these pages, you've gained insight into the world of public relations and the power it holds in shaping perceptions.

As I've shared my experiences with you, I want to stress the importance of authenticity in all public relations efforts. With the advancements in technology and social media, it's more important than ever to be genuine and transparent with your audience. People can see through gimmicks and empty promises, so it's important to build real relationships with your stakeholders.

I have also shared practical tips on how to craft a compelling message, connect with influencers, and navigate crises. These techniques can help businesses and individuals establish trust, credibility, and influence.

In closing, remember that public relations is a tool that can be used for good or ill – it's up to us to make sure we use it wisely. By prioritizing transparency, authenticity, and integrity in our communications efforts, we can build strong relationships that last a lifetime.

Thank you again for joining me on this journey. May your future public relations endeavors be filled with success!

ABOUT THE AUTHOR

Ray Goodwin

Ray Goodwin, is the author behind this series of captivating books on Business Development and self improvement, and has left an indelible mark on the field. He was born and raised in the bustling city of London, where he developed a strong work ethic and an insatiable curiosity about the inner workings of successful businesses. Throughout his illustrious career, Ray leveraged his extensive knowledge and experience to help numerous companies flourish and prosper.

His keen insights and innovative strategies has earned him recognition, driving him to share his expertise with others. Ray believes in the power of sharing knowledge to elevate businesses and empower aspiring entrepreneurs.

Ray's dedication to his craft is evident in the numerous books he has authored on business development and self improvement. His writing style seamlessly blends practical advice, thought-provoking concepts, and real-life case studies, making his books invaluable resources for business professionals and novices alike. His ability to distill complex concepts into accessible language has greatly impacted the lives and careers of countless individuals.

Now retired from the corporate world, Ray and his beloved wife have settled in the idyllic English countryside. Surrounded by the beauty of nature, Ray finds inspiration for his writing and indulges in his hobbies.

Ray Goodwin's books continue to serve as enduring guides for those seeking success in the business world. With a wealth of experience and a deep understanding of the inner workings of businesses, Ray's work remains a testament to his passion for sharing knowledge and helping others flourish.